CLASSROOM MANAGEMENT
for
Art, Music, and PE Teachers

Also by Michael Linsin

Dream Class

The Classroom Management Secret

Classroom Management for Art, Music, and PE Teachers

Michael Linsin

Printed in the USA

JME Publishing
San Diego, California
smartclassroommanagement.com

Copy Editor
Laura Decorte

Proofreader
Christine Haack

Illustrator
Rick Barnes

ISBN: 0615993265
ISBN: 978-0615993263

Table of Contents

Introduction

After many years as an elementary school classroom teacher, I decided to switch gears and become a physical education specialist. I was excited for the change, but knew I had a lot to learn. Classroom management, however, was one area I wasn't concerned about. After all, it was a great passion of mine. I had spent the previous 15 years studying and perfecting the strategies that would transform the widely disparate groups of students who showed up in my classroom every year into my dream class. To this day, I've written a couple of books on the topic and continue to publish weekly articles on my website, Smart Classroom Management.

But as I walked on campus the first time with a whistle around my neck, I was more than a little surprised to discover that what I knew to be true in the classroom wasn't necessarily true in the gym or on the playing field. Being a specialist teacher—that is, one who sees 500 or more students per week—is a singularly unique teaching experience, particularly when it comes to classroom management. It took me a couple of years to find my footing and a few more after that to attain the level of confidence I felt as a classroom teacher. What I learned along the way forms the contents of this book.

So why include art and music in the title? Well, although there are many elements of teaching physical education that are particular to physical education, and the same can be said of teaching art and music, the most effective classroom management approach is common to all three. In other words, the challenge is the same—and so are the solutions.

As you dig into the book and begin putting what you learn into practice, I think you'll find this to be the case. Furthermore, the tips, strategies, and solutions explained on the following pages are proven to work with all students from kindergarten through fifth grade. If you're a middle or high school teacher, I'm confident they'll work for you too. In fact, many of the strategies are offshoots of those I developed while teaching an outdoor education class to 7th, 8th, and 9th grade students over several summers many years ago.

One particular characteristic that I hope comes across is that the approach you're about to learn is simple. There aren't dozens and dozens of strategies you have to learn. You don't need any additional preparation time. And you'll always be respectful, kind, and honest with your students. The strategies are straightforward and have been tested over and over again and carefully whittled down to only what works and only what is doable for a real-world teacher. They're meant to save you time, lower your stress, and dramatically improve behavior, attentiveness, and motivation in every class you teach.

Are you ready? Let's get started!

Part One:
Leverage & Influence

Disadvantages

The biggest disadvantage to being a specialist teacher is that classroom teachers will always have more influence on your students. Despite your greatest efforts, the students that come to see you every week will be molded, good and bad, by their classroom teacher. So, for example, if they don't listen well in their own classroom, if they call out and interrupt their teacher, if they struggle to perform simple routines and procedures, then they'll bring those same behaviors with them when they see you.

Now, it's important to note that it's possible to attain a *level* of influence that extends from one week to the next, and we'll cover how in the coming chapters, but generally your students will arrive to your class week after week with the same habits they've learned in their home classroom. What this means is that unless you have the right mix of strategies to combat this phenomenon, you'll be at the mercy of your students and the classroom management skills and ability level of their teacher.

Unfortunately, that's not your only disadvantage. Like it or not, art, music, and PE don't have the same perceived level of importance as more traditional academic subjects. Your students may even view you as not quite a real teacher. After all, you don't conduct conferences, you don't assign homework, and you're not the leader who guides and directs them throughout each school day. Teachers, parents, and administrators also tend to view the arts as less relevant, particularly in this age of accountability and test scores. Sadly, this attitude comes across loud and clear to students.

So right out of the gate in many ways you have an uphill climb. And what can be especially frustrating is that few others on campus will recognize it. They may even assume that you have it easy because you *don't* see the same students every day. But the truth is, managing 20 or more classrooms per week with vastly different habits and personalities is the ultimate teaching challenge. Unless you're prepared, it's easy to get buried. It's easy to become overwhelmed and stressed and cynical about your job.

But it doesn't have to be this way. With the right classroom management approach, you can overcome these disadvantages. Regardless of how out of control and undisciplined your students appear when they arrive at your door, you can create the peaceful, well-behaved learning environment that you've always wanted. You can experience the deep fulfillment, quiet satisfaction, and unguarded freedom exceptional classroom management affords.

The first step is to become aware of your unique advantages.

Advantages

One of the keys to exceptional classroom management is to create a learning experience your students look forward to. The math is simple: If your students don't want to be there, then you'll have little if any leverage to influence their behavior. Consequences alone aren't enough, not even close. In this day and age, if you don't provide a compelling reason for your students to listen, attend, and actively participate, then your consequences won't carry any meaning or power to dissuade misbehavior, and you'll be destined to struggle week after week for control of your classroom.

The good news is that as an art, music, or PE teacher, your subject matter is inherently interesting. Without having to say a word, your students are already primed to look forward to your class. They've already experienced the pleasures of artistic and physical expression, from an early age, and the desire to learn and experience more comes naturally. This gives you a wonderful opening to capture their hearts. But you have to know how to take advantage of it. You have to know how to manage your classroom in such a way that allows you to highlight the extraordinary joys and rewards creative work offers while minimizing the disruptions that conspire to undermine it.

Another important advantage is that if you've decided to make teaching one particular subject area your life's work, then there was something about it that captivated you. There was something about playing music or being confronted with a masterpiece or participating in sports that enriched your life in a deep and meaningful way.

This passion, then, is inside of you. It need not be manufactured. By simply tapping into that part of yourself that first fell in love with your subject area, you'll naturally, effortlessly, draw students to you. They'll want to learn about watercolor painting or jazz music or basketball, for example, because the lesson is coming from someone who loves teaching it. Keeping that passion in the forefront, and not being afraid to express it, is a powerful first step in creating a class your students will look forward to and buzz about in the days leading up to seeing you.

It's common, however, for specialist teachers to get so bogged down with trying to manage behavior that they lose their passion. They lose that spark of charisma that lights up the room and enthralls their students. They feel so constrained by unruliness, so demoralized and hamstrung by interruptions, drama, and disrespect, that their goal shifts from boldly inspiring their students to just keeping a lid on the classroom. And it can happen quickly. Within 30 seconds of greeting your students it can feel like you're already behind the eight ball. It can feel like you've just jumped behind the wheel of a tractor-trailer with shoddy brakes, desperately pumping to avoid careening off course.

In the coming chapters you're going to learn simple strategies to pull that big rig under control, so you can be that inspiring teacher you've always wanted to be. And what's so exciting is that the more freedom you have to share your passion for art, music, or PE, the easier classroom management will become.

Relationships

You won't find much disagreement that building relationships with students is important. To a large degree it determines the amount of influence you have over their behavior choices. Conventional wisdom says that you build those relationships one student at a time, that you seek out and engage your students in personal and informal conversation, sharing likes and dislikes and comparing commonalities.

But getting to know anyone this way takes time; time a specialist teacher doesn't have. Given the sheer numbers of students you see every week, as well as the infrequency of your interactions, building relationships in this manner isn't realistic. Of course, there will always be those few students you have instant chemistry with, but for the majority of students, you'll never get to know them beyond a surface level.

There is also the question of whether a personal approach is indeed the best way to build influential relationships. I contend that it is not. In fact, even for classroom teachers, trying to build rapport one student at a time can be a mistake. You see, many students feel uncomfortable having personal conversations with adults—especially given awkward or unpleasant experiences they've had in the past. Their heart rate will increase. Their palms will perspire. They'll look down at their shoes, hem and haw, and whisper their responses. It can have the effect of pushing students away rather than drawing them near and into your circle of influence, especially if you're too familiar, too enthusiastic, or too gregarious, as many teachers are wont to be. It takes a subtle, highly nuanced, and skilled communicator to build rapport so personally.

The good news is that there is a better way, a way that doesn't take any additional time or extraordinary interpersonal skill. It's a strategy you can use whether you teach 30 students per week or 600. It doesn't matter who your students are, how old they are, or how uncomfortable they are interacting with adults. It doesn't even matter if they have an unfavorable view of teachers. It works reliably and isn't reliant on you forcing the relationship or trying to get to know your students on a personal level.

It's a strategy that attracts students to you and causes them to want to get to know you better. It causes them to want to listen and tune in to the sound of your voice. It's so powerful, in fact, that it even causes students to want to please you and behave for you, even when they don't behave for or in the presence of anyone else. So what is this miracle strategy?

It's simple, really. All you have to do is maintain a pleasant, friendly demeanor and the rest will take care of itself. If you can do this consistently, day-after-day, then powerful, behavior-influencing rapport with students will happen naturally and without you having to work at it. The catch, however, is that if you don't have solid classroom management skills, this can be a tall order. In the presence of an unruly and disruptive class, it can feel downright impossible. On this point, I ask that you bear with me. You see, affecting this attractive leadership quality works seamlessly with other principles and strategies in the book. In other words, what you'll learn the rest of the way, particularly about how best to respond to misbehavior, will make this strategy possible. It will free you to be the calm, friendly, and good-natured teacher your students will respect and admire.

In the meantime, know that no other strategy in the world will work as well in building positive and influential relationships with students. No other strategy will provide the leverage and power to change how students view you, respond to you, and behave while in your presence. And it comes effortlessly and highly predictably, no matter how many students you see every week.

Temperament

Your temperament has a profound effect on behavior, much more than most teachers realize. If ever you're stressed and uptight, about anything, then you'll bring a heaviness to your classroom or gymnasium your students will feel the moment they walk through your door. Even a general uneasiness about what the day may hold can be so powerful and disconcerting to students that it will cause them to become excitable, which is a major cause of misbehavior.

The kicker is that most teachers don't even realize they're doing it. They don't realize that their nervous energy is rubbing off on their students, that it's the very cause of all the movement and agitation, the loud voices and rambunctious behavior. The truth is, most teachers are perpetually tense, only letting down their guard when the last student leaves for the day. Because of this, chances are that many of the classes you service will arrive at your door already in this excitable state. They may be talkative and distracted. They may be restless and unable to keep their hands to themselves. They may be completely unprepared to even walk into your classroom. If you proceed as if this isn't the case, if you plow ahead expecting them to settle down on their own or after just a few reminders, then you're going to pay for it, with interest. Because it will only get worse.

Excitability is an issue specialist teachers need to take care of right away, before even allowing students to enter the classroom. In the Routines & Procedures section of the book, we'll cover precisely how to do this. We'll cover the first steps you should take the moment you take over for the class-room teacher. However, it is your own temperament that has the greatest effect on excitability. Your calm presence alone is enough to settle an excitable class, particularly after your students get to know you and become accustomed to the way you carry yourself.

You'll notice them visibly relax the moment they see you. Their shoulders will drop, their heads will stop swivel-ing about, and the tension will drain from their faces. Now, it's important to point out that if at any time you become nervous, worried, or tense, you'll soon see a reflection of your temperament in your students. They can go from relaxed and focused to excitable and distracted in a matter of seconds. So it's important that you maintain a calm but warm demeanor throughout each school day. This alone will allow you to avoid a mountain of headaches, make classroom management much easier, and free you to teach with far fewer interruptions or extremes in behavior.

It doesn't take much convincing for teachers to agree that their own stress and nervousness is a contributing factor to misbehavior. They can see it and feel it themselves, especially after experimenting with a day of maintaining a peaceful disposition. The difference is clear and often remarkable. But the tough part is how. How does one go about doing it day after day? How do you stay poised and self-assured when there are so many unknown variables? How do you remain composed when so much can and often does go wrong?

Well, there is a technique used by Olympic athletes who must remain relaxed despite chaos, uncertainty, and even danger whirling around them. It's a technique that allows them to concentrate on their responsibilities while remaining emotionally unaffected by variables out of their control. It's called the decide-first method, and it works just as well for teachers. It's a remarkably simple strategy that takes only a few minutes to put into action.

The way it works is that sometime before your first class arrives, find a quiet spot where you can sit or stand undisturbed. Once there, close your eyes and take a few long and slow deep breaths. Pause a moment and let the tension release from your body. What you're going to do now is make an important decision, followed by a promise to yourself. The decision you're going to make is to remain calm for the whole day *no matter what happens*. A herd of water buffaloes could stampede right through your class, but you'll stay as serene as a mountain lake. No matter the behavior, disruption, or unexpected surprise, you will not lose your composure. And guess what? You won't. Make this promise to yourself every day before greeting your first class and you'll be amazed at the results.

If it seems too easy, you're right. It is easy. But therein lies the beauty and power of the technique and the reason so many athletes swear by it. The other great thing about the technique is that it will work the first time you use it—and continue working as long as you adhere to the routine. In time, it will become a habit, a part of who you are and how you teach.

It's important to note that in no way do you have to temper your enthusiasm or curb your good humor. The idea is to stay calm and unruffled by negative behavior, disruptions, unruliness, and the like. It's not to remove all affectation. You're simply giving yourself permission, and your word, not to respond emotionally to drama, what ifs, circular thoughts, worries, anxieties, or stress of any kind. Keeping an even keel regardless of what happens in your class or the behaviors you witness is a characteristic of the most effective specialist teachers. You'll do well to follow their example.

Composure

The biggest mistake you can make as a specialist teacher is losing your cool in response to misbehavior. Yelling, scolding, lecturing, and the like undermine your relationship with your students, making it much harder to manage your classroom. Remember, if your students don't like you, trust you, and look forward to being in your class, then you'll have little if any leverage to influence their behavior. The truth is, nothing causes more hurt and resentment and a rejection of your teaching than taking out your frustrations on your students. It can even cause them to willfully exact revenge in the form of more frequent and more severe misbehavior.

It's an easy habit to fall into because there is a measure of release, a feeling of getting your frustration and dissatisfaction off your chest. It can also cause a temporary cessation of misbehavior and induce immediate compliance. But it's a huge price to pay. Behavior changes only when students want to change, which is a result of fair and consistent accountability combined with a teacher students like and trust.

Taking misbehavior personally and using intimidation to force students into obedience will backfire on you every time. It will cause them to dislike you intensely and take pleasure in misbehaving behind your back. Add a consequence to the equation, like time-out for example, and instead of sitting quietly and reflecting on their misbehavior, they'll be seething in anger at you. All their energy will be focused on their resentment of you and the perceived unfairness of the consequence, which is no accountability at all.

The solution, which we'll cover more fully in Part Four, is to calmly follow a previously taught and agreed upon classroom management plan. A student misbehaves and you enforce a consequence. It's that simple. And because it isn't personal, because you follow your plan dispassionately and regardless of who breaks a rule, your students will take responsibility for their actions. They'll ponder and reflect on their mistakes and resolve to do better. They'll know, without you having to spell it out for them, that the consequence they received is a result of their own doing. They may not be happy about it, but they'll know that it isn't personal. This ensures that your positive relationship with your students remains intact and influential.

Mixing rules and consequences with talking-tos, finger-wagging lectures, and admonishments is one of the reasons so many specialist teachers struggle with classroom management. Every warning and every time-out becomes a battle, with both sides annoyed and angry and determined to get the better of the other.

Once you create a classroom management plan and teach it thoroughly to your students, it becomes a promise that says that you will follow it to the letter without adding your hurtful two cents or replacing it with a rip-roaring dressing down. This places the burden of responsibility squarely on the shoulders of your students, with none of it clinging to you. This doesn't mean your students will never be angry about going to time-out. What it means is that they'll know in their heart that it was their doing.

Letting your classroom management plan do the dirty work for you also removes oceans of stress from your teaching life. It eliminates the feeling of wanting to get even with students or put them in their place. It also saves you from trying to find the right words or the right lecture to try and convince or coerce your students into behaving. The guesswork is removed. You know exactly what to do in response to every incident of misbehavior and are able to do it quickly and without drama.

Room Environment

A disorderly classroom or teaching area is an invitation for students to misbehave. They take one look around and, seeing clutter, disorganization, and untidiness, assume that expectations must not be very high. In other words, if the teacher doesn't take pride in the room's appearance, then it's unlikely they're going to be much of a stickler when it comes to behavior, work habits, performance, and the like. And the truth is, they're right. It's exceedingly rare to find a classroom where the environment says one thing while student behavior says another, which makes it a remarkably accurate predictor of teacher effectiveness.

The physical representation of your classroom is such an important influencer that if you let it fall into disorder, even a little, then it will have a negative effect on behavior. It will make your most passionate and sincere call for politeness and respect seem vacant and insincere. It will make the words you use and the lessons you teach less weighty, less meaningful, and less worthy of your students' attention.

By the same token, an attractive, organized classroom whispers to all who enter that good behavior and work habits are expected. It causes students and visitors alike to enter your room like they're walking into a museum, with a sense of reverence and decorum. It matches your message of respect— for you, for each other, and for the materials, instruments, and equipment used in your lessons. Although by itself an attractive classroom won't change behavior, it will make your expectations congruent with what your students see around them. It will communicate in no uncertain terms that you mean what you say, that you walk the talk.

It's important to point out that there is a difference between a classroom environment that supports creativity and one that is sloppy and unappealing. Your room doesn't have to be austere or drab, it just needs to reflect your expectations. The good news is that although initially it may take some work to get your classroom, music room, or gymnasium in ship-shape, particularly at the start of a new school year, it's a responsibility you can then turn over to your students. In fact, including a brief clean up as part of a routine at the end of every class period will help ingrain a sense of pride in their work and the greater good of the classroom.

Maintaining an organized and attractive room environment is a simple little thing, but it means so much. It commands instantaneous respect. It encourages politeness and responsibility. It alights your classroom in the unmistakable glow of excellence.

Praise

P raise is a tricky area for art, music, and PE teachers because some students will have more immediate natural
ability than others. This can be true of academic subjects as
well, but to a less prominent, less outwardly obvious degree.
When you praise students for work or performance they're
inherently good at, particularly if it's too enthusiastic, it can
have the effect of freezing them up and placing undue pres-
sure on them to perform. They can become so wrapped up in
their identity as gifted, special, talented, etc. that it can cause
them to be afraid to fail, afraid to take chances, and afraid to
make mistakes, all of which are critical to their development
as artists, musicians, and athletes.

It can also cause them to overestimate their abilities, re-
sulting in painful realizations later on down the line. The other
issue is that of the other students—those who are of average
ability or who struggle just to learn the basics. If you seek to
praise them equally, they can take a look around at their classmates effortlessly producing better work and conclude that

it isn't genuine. Despite outward reactions to the contrary, if your praise isn't legitimate and worthy, deep down your students will know it.

The solution is to praise your students based on effort and individual progress, which is different for every student, less associated with identity, and unequivocally praiseworthy. This will encourage them to continue working to improve their skills, regardless of how advanced or rudimentary their level. It will also encourage them to take risks and push the boundaries of their capabilities. You can and should still give your students honest, targeted feedback on their work, which may include using words such as beautiful and excellent, but it should never be linked to who they are. As in, "You're amazing!" Nor should it be confused with praise. Praise provides the fuel to keep them moving forward while feedback keeps them on the right course.

Now, it's important to separate praise given in response to work and performance and praise given for expected behavior. Too many teachers tell students how wonderful they are because they sat attentively during a lesson, lined up quietly for lunch, or *didn't* argue during an activity, but what this does is communicate that somehow doing what is minimally required is an accomplishment worthy of special recognition. It lowers the bar of excellence and undermines that which is truly worthy of praise. A better way to let students know they performed a common expectation well is to simply thank them for it.

There are exceptions, which may include learning a new routine, students with special needs, and difficult students who've just accomplished a behavior-related goal.

Praising students for exceptional effort or attainment of a new level of skill takes a keen eye and a subtle touch. As teachers we have been conditioned to believe that the more enthusiastic and animated the praise is, the more effective it will be. But the reality is, in most cases, the opposite is true. A private, sincere interaction between teacher and student has more intrinsic value than does the public, over-the-top variety, especially if the teacher is someone the student trusts and admires. Eye contact and a head nod from across the room, a knowing smile, a whispered, "I knew you could do it" . . . these genuine, heartfelt moments can mean the world to students.

Done right, praise can ignite that burning intrinsic motivation that spurs better performance, sharper attention to detail, and a greater desire to learn, take chances, and grow as artists and athletes. But you must be on the lookout for effort beyond the ordinary. You must eschew false praise and praise based on common behavior expectations. You must provide feedback that is specific, helpful to future performance, and never confused with praise. You must be real and sincere and willing to be a teacher whose words and gestures will be remembered for a lifetime.

Lessons

To create the leverage and influence you need to curb even the most challenging behavior, you must offer your students more than simply the inherent interest of your subject area. Teaching art, music, or PE may give you a leg up on your classroom-teaching counterparts, but by themselves they're not enough to create the well-behaved learning environment you really want. You have to give your students something more. You have to send them on their way after their hour with you happily shaken and with something to talk about.

As was mentioned in a previous chapter, it's important that your students look forward to coming to your class every week. This is what gives your classroom management plan its teeth. You see, if your students enjoy being in your class, then they won't want to waste even a second of their time withering away in time-out. This is what is meant by having leverage, and the more leverage you have the more peaceful your classroom will be.

Much of your leverage will come from you—your warm and friendly personality, your trustworthiness, your consistency, and your leadership presence. But outside of creating influential relationships, the most important area is your lesson. As a specialist teacher, your one lesson per week is all you have. You have far fewer, if any, opportunities to create leverage with your students. Thus, that one lesson must be somehow noteworthy. It must resonate with your students and stay with them after they leave your room.

The best way to make this a reality is to look for the most compelling aspect of each lesson you plan and highlight it for your students. What will they find most interesting, fascinating, or unusual about what you're going to show them? Whatever it is, you'll want to make it the focal point of your lesson.

You'll still provide the information your students need to fulfill the objective, but you're going to *sell* what is most compelling. For example, in PE most of our objectives can be put into practice through a culminating game or activity. Typically, I teach a skill and then incorporate that skill into a larger game. Now, between you and me, many of the games aren't terribly exciting, but because they form the core of what we do, I have to make them exciting. It's the one thing that gets my students happily through much of the hard work we do improving strength and fitness to start the period. It's the one thing that can keep even the most difficult student attentive and out of time-out.

So what's the best way to sell a lesson? You *show* your students how and why it's cool and worth learning. So many teachers just . . . teach, but never let their students know why what they're learning is worth learning. They don't sell it. They don't use their enthusiasm, their passion, or their humor to show their students how gnarly or scary or fun or super cool it is to make coil pots, play Hot Cross Buns on a recorder, or throw a Frisbee through a rolling hula hoop.

And this makes all the difference. This is what gets students excited, sitting up straight, and wanting to learn. This is what keeps them focused and interested. Along with your classroom management plan, this is what gives you the leverage you need, week after week, to create the teaching and learning experience you really want.

Points

The very best classroom teachers work to extend their influence beyond the four walls of their classroom. These are the teachers you can count on, year after year, to produce students who are prepared to listen and follow your directions. Not surprisingly, they want to know, sometimes in great detail, any behavior issues you're having with their class. This is wonderful, of course, because a second layer of accountability makes your job easier. However, discussing behavior with classroom teachers is an area you have to be careful with. You never want to give the impression that you're complaining or in any way intimating that how their students behave when they're with you is their responsibility. It's not. It's yours, fully and completely.

One solution is to provide your feedback via a point system based on four definable whole-group expectations:

1 point for entering class quietly.
1 point for listening attentively.

1 point for good effort.

1 point for lining up to leave quietly.

The brief descriptions can be interpreted in a number of ways, so it's critical that you define for your students precisely what each one means and what standard must be met to earn each point. You'll also want to model and practice thoroughly before putting the strategy into practice. In a short amount of time, though, both you and they will know beyond any doubt which points were earned and which were not. At the end of each class period when their teacher comes to pick them up, you simply announce how many points they earned for the hour. *"You earned a three today. You lost your listening point because when I asked for your attention, I had to wait for you to give it to me."*

The point system is easy to manage and has several advantages beyond just providing feedback. It also rallies students to work together as they try to earn their points each week. And if you make a grade-level competition out of it, it gently encourages *all* of your classroom teachers to try and extend their influence beyond their classroom. The result is that your students will be better prepared when they show up at your door.

It's up to you to determine how many points a class needs to earn to be recognized as the top class in the grade level. However, 30 points seems about right. It allows for the competition to heat up, but at the same time the number feels doable to students. Once you have a winning class, you can present them with a modest handmade poster that identifies them as such. They can put it on their classroom door or up on the wall if they wish. This isn't something you need to make a big deal out of. In fact, it's best if you don't.

Bribing students to behave in return for rewards sends the wrong message and interferes with the unsullied joy of being a participating member of your class. Therefore, it's important to make clear that your students will not be receiving anything beyond the simple acknowledgement that they were the best class over a period of time. It's the teamwork, the bragging rights, and the intrinsic pride of being part of a sharp, well-behaved class that is the real award and lesson of earning points.

It's important to note that the point system is meant for the class as a whole and that no individual student, no matter how disruptive, should affect the number of points given. Also, during weeks when there is a holiday and no school, the best way to handle it is to simply tell each class that although you'll still report the number of points earned to their teacher, you won't record them, because it isn't fair to those classrooms you were unable to see that week. Your students will understand and try to do well just the same. You won't notice any difference in behavior as a result.

Finally, it's a mistake to assume that this one strategy is enough to create the well-behaved classes you want. Effective classroom management is a result of the full complement of strategies you'll find in this book. The points strategy merely adds a measure of teamwork, competition, and group accountability that reinforces and supports the other strategies.

Part Two:
Routines & Procedures

The Purpose of Routines

Routines are among the most important strategies a specialist teacher can use because they make *everything* easier. Anything and everything you do repeatedly as a class—entering the classroom, collecting materials, cleaning up, etc.— should be made into a routine your students can do with little or no input from you. This saves you oceans of time, cuts way down on misbehavior, and helps your students stay focused on learning.

Routines also keep your class moving forward briskly, from and through one transition, activity, and lesson to the next. They help you instill in your students a sense of purpose. A busy classroom, after all, is a productive and well-behaved one, and routines play a crucial role in ensuring that it remains that way.

A class that is unable to enter your classroom or activity area in the same quiet, composed way every week is unlikely to be prepared to listen, learn, and get down to business. They'll be distracted and fidgety and will need your threats, warnings, and reminders before being ready to learn. By utilizing an entering-the-classroom routine, however, they'll already be settled, focused, and goal-driven by the time they sit down. Beginning the period with a well-taught routine also helps shake them from any malaise or excitability they may have picked up before showing up at your door. It tells them that it's time to get to work fulfilling a responsibility. And if they know that a point is riding on the first routine, it centers and prepares them even sharper for your lesson.

Not everything can be made into a routine, of course. But for everything repeatable, there should be a standard and highly specific way of doing it. This doesn't mean that routines must be militaristic or robotic. It just means that there is a detailed expectation of how each routine should be completed. You can make them as fun or as interesting or as casual as you wish. In fact, as we'll see in the next chapter, when you add steps to a routine, even nonsensical steps, it makes the routine more memorable and your students more motivated to perform it as taught.

Routines improve behavior because they keep idleness to a minimum. Students move from one area or transition to the next with far fewer opportunities to misbehave. Furthermore, because their minds are engaged performing the routine as specified, misbehavior is less likely to even occur to them. Boredom is driven away the moment they enter your classroom. They go directly from routine to lesson to routine to activity and back again until the final routine, when they're waiting in line for their teacher.

One of the most common complaints from specialist teachers is that they have to talk their students through *everything*, from the moment the students arrive until the moment they leave. With routines, however, this is never the case. Your students already know how to enter your classroom, line up, sit on the rug, gather materials, etc., without you having to walk or talk them through it. Your only job, then, is to observe.

The final benefit of routines is that they transfer. The focus required to perform a routine with excellence will transfer to your lessons and activities. They help create an association between your classroom and doing things the right way, between your classroom and success, and between your classroom and a love of learning.

Teaching Routines

The secret to teaching memorable routines is to make them highly detailed—much more detailed than you're probably used to. You have to *show* your students from start to finish precisely and explicitly what you want them to do, and in a way that makes sense to them. This is important for classroom teachers, to be sure. For specialists, however, despite having far fewer routines to teach, it's absolutely critical because it so directly affects behavior and the success you have delivering your lessons.

The first three to four weeks of the school year, you'll want to spend up to half of each period both on teaching routines and your classroom management plan. Remember, for every repeatable moment, week after week, there should be a routine. For example, every class must enter your classroom. Therefore, how you want them to enter should be made into a routine. The best place to start teaching a routine is wherever they are in the moments before the routine is to begin. So if you're teaching your students how to enter your classroom, you would take them outside to the very spot you meet them before walking in.

The first step is to simply model what you want. The key here is that you pretend that you are an actual student, performing the routine as expected. Put yourself in their shoes—sitting at their desks, standing in their lines, putting away their equipment. Allow your students to circle around you as you model for them what you expect, leaving nothing out and nothing to chance. You can narrate as you progress through each step along the way.

I recommend even adding a step or two. The more detailed you can make the routine, the more memorable it will be. A routine like entering the classroom can be so mundane that an additional step like tapping a poster on the wall before sitting down can help put them in a more focused, more purposeful frame of mind. The first routine sets the tone, gets them in the habit of doing what you ask, and enables them to feel successful right off the bat.

The second step is to model what you *don't* want. Show them the most common misbehaviors you witness when students come into your classroom—or gather materials, form groups, participate in class, etc. This can be remarkably effective, especially if you exaggerate the unwanted behavior. As long as it doesn't appear you're making fun of any one student, it's okay to have fun with it. It's okay if your students laugh and nod their heads knowingly. You'll find that few students will repeat whatever misbehaviors you model in detail.

The final step is to practice. First choose one student to model in the exact same way you did during the initial step. Observe carefully to make sure it is the same in every way. If anything is amiss, point it out and then have the student try again. Next, have a couple more students try the routine. The reason for this is not only so your students see that the routine can be done well by a fellow student, but also because it gives you feedback regarding how well they understood your modeling. You never want to move on to whole-class practice until you know for certain that you taught the routine well enough for your students to understand. Once you're satisfied with your individual modelers, then allow the whole class to practice. When they prove they can do it without your guidance, it's time to let them perform it as part of a normal school day.

You may have a class test you the moment you try the routine for the first time. In all likelihood your students have had teachers in the past who have taught routines as thoroughly as you, but then dropped the ball thereafter. In fact, few teachers actually stick to their original expectations. To be successful, to have the well-behaved classes you desire, you must stick to the same standard of excellence day after day. This first time your students perform a routine for real is especially important.

Keeping your expectations through the roof sends the message that you really do expect them to walk in without a sound and tap the "Learn Like A Champion" poster on the wall. It sends the message that you expect excellence in everything they do. If they fail to perform this or any routine as taught, then immediately send them back to do it again.

Arrival

When your students arrive for your class, it's important that you meet them outside the door of your classroom or activity area. This is essential to ensuring good listening and proper behavior throughout the entire period. Because of the varying degrees of behavior expectations among classroom teachers, as well as other variables, you'll never really know what you're going to get from your students from week to week. Thus, you mustn't assume that any class will arrive ready to listen and learn.

The first few seconds or so are best spent assessing how much or how little prepared they are to enter your classroom. As you're doing this, stand silently and wait for them to form a quiet line in the manner you taught them as part of your initial routine. So many specialist teachers run into trouble because they get ahead of themselves. They rush their students along, all the while ignoring the signs that the period is unlikely to go well.

One of the keys to effective classroom management is to never move on until you're getting exactly what you want from your students, and it starts the second they arrive. Let them dictate how fast you proceed based on their behavior. The idea is to move from one moment, transition, routine, or instruction to the next seamlessly and successfully, no matter how long it takes. If you stick to this principle, you'll discover each class getting better, sharper, faster, and more prepared to learn as the weeks go by. Without this principle, however, you'll rarely find yourself gaining any traction. You'll rarely see much improvement in behavior from one week to the next.

As soon as you have their attention, it's time to employ what is called the preview strategy, which is the first step to "selling" your lesson. The preview strategy is meant to get your students excited about what they're going to learn that day. The idea is to build anticipation by explaining the one thing that is unique, exciting, fun, mysterious, or otherwise noteworthy about your lesson. There is always something. It's often as simple as articulating what it is about your subject that is so compelling to you. You won't necessarily reveal what the lesson entails, but you'll explain what's in it for them. You're giving them reason to *want* to listen and behave and hear what you have to teach them.

There is no need to go on and on. Your preview should only take a minute or two. When you finish, there is one more thing you must do before sending them into your classroom. Now that you have their attention, now that they're motivated to get started, you must remind them of your classroom management plan (Part Four). You must remind them that if they don't follow the music class rules, for example, they could miss some or all of the awesome lesson you have planned.

The double-barrel motivation of wanting to learn combined with the prospect of missing out on something really cool will eliminate most of the behavior problems and issues that plague so many specialist teachers. After another short pause, give your signal for them to begin the first routine of entering the room and sitting down quietly.

Transitions

Transitions start with whatever signal you use to call for your students' attention. It can be a whistle if you're a PE teacher or a simple, "Can I have your attention please?" Bells and tones also work as well. I don't recommend counting down from five—which is a threat with no consequence on the other side—or having your students repeat your words ("One, two, three, eyes on me!") or number of handclaps—which for specialist teachers can lead to more disruption.

The key with getting their attention immediately is to practice. Let them talk or have fake conversations and then practice giving your signal until they can stop, turn, and look at you silently within a couple of seconds. If ever they don't give you their attention right away, just wait until they do. Refrain from giving your signal again. Over time this will help ingrain the habit of turning their attention away from their work and toward you as soon as possible. Reminding them of the possibility of losing a point is also effective.

Asking for attention can be a challenge because it so directly reflects how things are done in their home classroom. If their teacher doesn't have a similarly high expectation for giving respectful attention, then they'll come to you with the same tendency to ignore your signal. The key, though, again, is to wait. It's likely that the reason they aren't quiet and respectful is because their classroom teacher moves on without having everyone's attention. If you, on the other hand, hold them to it by waiting, then in time they'll become better and better—especially if you have a great activity waiting in the wings. The big mistake is giving in and moving on, which merely reinforces the bad habit.

The success of the next step is contingent on how well you provide your students with directions and whether you consistently hold them accountable for following them. We'll cover exactly how to do this in Part Three, but in the meantime you'll want to model in detail how you want them to transition. If it's one of the same transitional routines you rely on every week, like cleaning up, for example, then you don't have to model it again. If there is any change, however, or if you're transitioning in a way your students are unaccustomed to, then it always pays to model what you want.

After checking for understanding and asking if there is anyone who *doesn't* know what to do—which is a technique that effectively shifts the burden of responsibility from you to your students—you'll give your signal for them to begin and then verify that your directions are followed to a tee. If they're not, then without complaining or pointing out how poorly they did, send them back to do it again. As a specialist teacher, it's your consistency in being specific with your expectations, and then holding students accountable for following them, that ultimately will make a difference from one week to the next.

It's the only way for transitions to be smooth and efficient despite what may or may not be happening in the home classroom. Your sameness week after week can overcome the most difficult and undisciplined class of students. It's when you let things go, when good enough becomes good enough, that trouble follows and chaos ensues.

Dismissal

To instill in your students the understanding that when they're with you there is a high standard of behavior, you must finish each class period as purposefully and orderly as it began. So often specialists will begin the period strong enough, but then gradually lose control as the minutes tick by. A well-taught, well-modeled finishing routine bookends a solid start and keeps students sharp, on-task, and focused throughout.

Much like the arrival routine, your dismissal routine should begin with silence. As covered in the previous chapter, your students must be able to give you their quiet attention whenever you ask for it. The only way to make sure this happens is to model and practice it thoroughly as part of the series of classroom management-related lessons you'll conduct during the first few weeks of the school year.

After asking for their attention, pause 30 seconds or so to let any residual excitement in the air dissipate. Just relax and breathe and allow them a moment to toggle their attention away from their work and toward you and your impending message.

Your final routine should be devoted to cleaning up the room or activity area and putting materials away. Because the specifics may vary from week to week, it's important that you detail for your students precisely what you want them to do. Using language that is both simple and unambiguous, you're going to tell them step by step the areas and items that need their attention. You'll model *how* you want them to clean up in the beginning of the school year, but from week to week you'll merely announce what you want completed.

After reminding your students that a point is riding on this final routine, and after another brief pause, give your signal to begin and then watch closely. If there is going to be a problem with misbehavior, it will likely occur within the first 10 seconds. If you see anything amiss, stop your class immediately, return them to the beginning of the routine, and then start again. If you let it go, then their behavior will worsen all the way up until you release them to their classroom teacher. Furthermore, it will continue to worsen the following week. Remember, you never want to move on until you're getting exactly what you want from your students. Whenever you forget this key principle, it comes back to haunt you.

As they're cleaning up and putting items away, your only job is to observe and make sure it's done as you ask. Try to avoid offering reminders or talking your students through the clean up. This is a common mistake that actually has the opposite of the intended effect. The more you jump in and do for your students what they can do for themselves, the more dependent they'll become. Before long, you'll find yourself doing most of the work. Learned helplessness can sneak up on you quickly if you're not careful.

I recommend finishing the dismissal routine in a straight, quiet line, where your students can await your rendering of how many points they've earned for the day. Once clean up is completed give them 30 seconds or so to form a line. It's okay and healthy for them to politely remind and jostle each other into line. When leaders emerge and take ownership of the class and the points they earn, it encourages and empowers the whole group to get better. The final benefit of an end-of-period routine is that you can hand them off to their class-room teacher in the same calm, ready-to-learn state week after week.

Group Accountability

One of the great benefits of routines is that the team-work, focus, and discipline required to do them well transfers to everything you do. If your students are able to enter your classroom, circle into groups, or clean their instruments with efficiency and purpose, then they'll be better able to fulfill the many other tasks, goals, and challenges you place before them. Routines send a message of excellence that reaches into every corner of your classroom. But it only works if you hold them to the same standard by which you first taught them. It only works if you hold them accountable whenever a routine strays from your expectations.

If a routine is performed poorly and you let it go without a response, you send the unmistakable message to your students that you don't really mean what you say—which also transfers to everything you do. This is a common mistake and a chief reason why so many teachers struggle to get students to perform even basic routines. They teach the routine well enough, but somewhere along the line they start accepting less than the original expectation. Before long, routines aren't the only thing affected. The downward spiral of standards, behavior, and respect become part of the very climate of your classroom.

Another common mistake is reacting emotionally to a poorly followed routine—to rant, lecture, and admonish students when they mess up. But this is a time-consuming, stressful way to manage your classroom. It also causes resentment and undermines your desire to create a classroom your students like and want to be a part of. Intimidation may indeed work in the short term, but the long-term cost is much too steep.

A better way to handle a bad routine is to simply stop your students in their tracks at the first sign of trouble, send them back to where the routine began, and have them do it again. It's fast, effective, and sends the message you want: that you expect excellence in everything they do. It also protects your relationship with your students, allowing you to hold them accountable without causing ill will.

Effective classroom management is about action. It's not about intimidation, coercion, or trying to bribe or convince your students to behave. It's teaching and modeling a standard of behavior that is optimal for learning and then holding your students to that standard. There is great misunderstanding among teachers of all stripes that somehow you have to show your displeasure when students misbehave or fail to live up to your expectations, that you have to feign anger or display frustration or verbalize your disappointment. But it isn't true. In fact, you'll be much more effective if you keep your composure and your criticisms to yourself. You'll be much more effective if you hold your students accountable calmly, even pleasantly.

So instead of getting riled up or trying to rely on your powers of persuasion, let your actions speak for you. Simply send your students back to perform the routine again. Then move on with your day without a second thought.

Time Management

Not having enough time for classroom management is a common complaint from specialist teachers. With only 45 minutes to an hour per class, thoroughly teaching your routines and procedures, let alone your classroom management plan, can feel like a daunting challenge. Especially given that you don't want to completely ignore your curriculum. Part of getting your students onboard and buying into your program is making sure that you're teaching interesting lessons, projects, and activities right from the beginning, the first week if possible.

The good news is that when it comes to effective classroom management, there isn't *that* much you need to teach, especially when compared to a classroom teacher. One of the goals of this book is to streamline classroom management for you, to simplify it and make it doable despite the time constraints. Thus, you'll only find what is proven to work in a real-world classroom, music room, or gymnasium. Anything and everything that is ineffective, needless, or unethical has been left on the cutting room floor.

The other thing to remember is that, in most cases, you only have to teach your routines and classroom management plan once. When done right the first time, you save hours and hours of time over the course of a school year that you may otherwise have spent lecturing, enduring distractions, repeating poorly followed directions, and so on. Effective classroom management saves time. It never wastes it.

As mentioned in an earlier chapter, you'll want to spend half of the first three or four class sessions teaching, modeling, and practicing your routines and your classroom management plan. The rest of the time can be devoted to a short project or activity. From year to year, though, because you'll have most of the same students in your class, you can realistically knock out all your classroom management-related lessons in just two class periods, no problem. This doesn't include, however, when you feel a particular class needs a refresher or when you may want to review key points of your plan after a holiday break.

Another consideration is that if your students can do one routine well, then the rest of the routines come much easier. Once they understand where your standard is, then it's just a matter of knowing what to do. The key takeaway for students is not so much the routine itself, but that you expect all directions to be followed in the same way they're taught. Once this point is made using the first routine you teach as a vehicle, then it's established. Your only job then becomes holding them to it.

Although there is an initial time investment, routines are the lifeblood of effective specialist teaching. They help students stay focused, out of trouble, and purpose driven. They keep your class running smoothly. And they allow you to do so much more with your students. You can teach that cool but involved art project. You can take that next step with your music class. You can move the mere practice of lacrosse out to the playing fields for a real game. Put simply, you have more time to teach and your students have more time to learn.

Part Three:
Listening & Following Directions

Voice/Speaking

One of the most powerful classroom management tools you have is your voice, but few teachers give it much thought. They just dive in and speak in whatever way comes naturally, never making the connection between their verbal habits and the poor behavior and inattentiveness that plague their class. By making simple adjustments to your tone, volume, frequency, and pace you can substantially affect how well your students listen and behave.

The first and most critical area to examine is your tone. Students feed off your energy, and if you're nervous, tense, or in a hurry, it will come through in your voice and manifest itself in excitability among your students. Excitability is a major cause of misbehavior, but it can be avoided simply by speaking in a calmer, more easygoing tone. This doesn't mean that you must be stiff or monotone when addressing your class. It just means that speaking in a calm voice will become your default setting. It will be your dominant manner of speaking when giving directions, providing information, or managing your classroom. You'll still present your lessons with passion. You'll still use your voice to help motivate and inspire. But only after assessing that you have your students' full attention and only while in the midst of a high-interest lesson.

Most teachers also tend to talk too loud, believing that the higher the volume the more likely students will listen. But the opposite is true. As long as your students can hear you, it pays to speak softly. Raising your voice sounds like nagging or threatening to students. The unpleasantness discourages them from listening and tuning in to the sound of your voice. It discourages them from following you with their eyes and concentrating on your meaning. On the other hand, when you lower your voice, your students will become still. They'll stop fidgeting and tapping. They'll turn toward you rather than away from you. They'll lean in and actively read your non-verbal clues. Furthermore, the information goes down a lot smoother. It sounds polite and respectful. It sounds like you believe in them and their ability. It makes them *want* to listen.

Talking too much is also a common mistake. When you talk too much, what you say has less impact and takes on less meaning and relevance for students. The endless reminders, warnings, asides, and parenthetical statements wear students out and cause them to turn their attention elsewhere. Being more mindful of how often you speak, however, and ensuring that every word counts, will make you more interesting and your words more compelling. Most teachers who talk too much also tend to repeat themselves, sometimes repeating every sentence two, three, and four times. But what this does is train students *not* to listen. You see, if they know that you'll always repeat yourself, then there is no reason to listen to you the first time.

It's easy to fall into the trap of rushing to get your directions and instructions out to students, especially in the early minutes of a class period, but talking too fast causes you to run one sentence into the next without adequate pause. Students need frequent and sometimes extended pauses to download the information you're giving them. They need a chance to visualize what you're asking of them and consider possible questions or obstacles. Frequent pausing also builds suspense, encourages predictions, adds depth and drama, helps students retain information, and gives you a chance to check in and assess their understanding.

As a specialist teacher without benefit of having the same group of students every day, you need to take advantage of the many simple strategies that can have profound effect on behavior and attentiveness. The way you speak to your students, particularly when providing directions and general information, is one such example. These small changes alone can be a difference-maker. All things being equal, a teacher with good speaking skills will experience greater success, better behavior, and a more polite and attentive class than one who speaks in whatever way comes naturally.

Simple First

It's common for specialist teachers to struggle getting students to follow directions. It's yet another downside to seeing your students only once per week. You may very well have excellent lessons on the topic of listening, but because so much time passes between class sessions, it's difficult to ingrain good habits. Furthermore, your students may be learning a completely different set of, ahem, listening habits from their classroom teacher. This is why each week it can feel like you're seeing them for the very first time.

The solution to this problem isn't to teach your students *how* to listen, which doesn't have staying power from one week to the next. The solution is in the way you give a direction, which, done correctly, will groove the listening habits you want. Over the next few chapters we're going to cover four unique strategies that can train even your most difficult students to listen and follow your directions the first time you give them.

The first strategy is about as easy as it gets, but the best thing about it is that it will work the first time you use it as well as every time thereafter. It's a strategy you can count on again and again whenever you sense distraction or restlessness in your students. It's called the simple-first strategy. The idea is to get your students following simple, one step directions first before slowly increasing the complexity until they're listening and doing what you ask with speed and precision.

For example, let's say you're dealing with an especially challenging class. You've tried a few basic directions, but with little success. Eventually they may follow them, but not without wasting time or causing considerable trouble. Some even sit in their seats daydreaming and unaware of their surroundings until it dawns on them that the other students are moving and performing tasks. Once one direction is completed it takes you another few minutes just to settle them down long enough to give a follow up direction.

The best way to handle this situation is to start over with an unrelated direction so simple and so demonstrative that they can't help but follow it. For example, you might say simply, "Stand up," and then wait until everyone is standing before then saying, "Sit down." After asking them to stand again—and perhaps even sit down again—you might say something like, "Place one hand on your head." After waiting until everyone is in the correct position, you would continue: "Put your hands on your waist . . . Point to the teacher . . . Stand on one leg and nod your head . . . Clap your hands twice, sit down, and look at me . . . etc." You're going to slowly work your students into the habit of precisely following your directions, increasing complexity as you go.

Once you're satisfied with how well they're performing, you can either slip in the first real direction you want them to follow, or you can simply begin your lesson. Either way, you'll find your students more focused, more engaged, and more prepared to learn. The strategy literally trains them on the spot to be good listeners, and you'll find that their sharp attentiveness and efficient performance will continue for the rest of the hour. If not, however, you can always just begin again, "Raise one hand in the air . . . cross your arms . . ."

You don't have to wait until noticing how poorly your students are listening to employ the simple-first strategy. It can also be used proactively at the very beginning of your class period. The other nice benefit of the strategy is that it doesn't take long. It takes no explanation or pre-planning. And you never have to just stand there helpless, hoping they'll get better. You just jump in with a simple direction and off you go. Within just a couple of minutes your class should be ready to listen and learn. However, you can always extend the training session if you need to.

The main purpose of the simple-first strategy is to get your students listening and following your directions effectively so you can get on with the business of teaching. It's meant to fix the problem on the spot and in the moment. However, when it's used along with the rest of the strategies described in Part Three, it can groove listening habits to such a degree that your students will show up to your class prepared to learn—even if they're not that way for their classroom teacher. Now, granted, with some classes this is less likely. But at the very least you'll be able to whip them into shape quickly, no matter how unprepared or distracted they are when they show up at your door.

Giving a Direction

A lot of misbehavior can be avoided simply by giving directions in a way students can understand, both in your expectations for what they need to do and in how you want them to do it. In this regard, it pays to leave nothing to chance. It pays to paint a complete picture for your students, one in which they can see themselves successfully completing the tasks, challenges, and responsibilities you ask of them.

It starts with the lengthy pause we covered a couple of chapters ago to ensure your students are ready to listen. Half the battle is won by simply waiting, observing their body language, and assessing that they're indeed attentive before opening your mouth. Moving on too soon is a common mistake that is difficult to recover from.

The first words out of your mouth should be the phrase, "In a moment," as in "In a moment you're going to open your song books." What this does is stop your students from moving on mentally or physically before you've finished speaking, which is the number one reason students don't listen well.

They think they already know what you want, so they tune out everything else you say. 'In a moment,' stops them in their tracks. It tells them that there is more they need to hear.

Next, you're going to create a visualization—or movie in their mind—of precisely what you want them to do. The best way to do this is to use 'you' and 'going to' language. (Example: "*You're going to* stand up, walk over to the materials table, and pick up your watercolor tray. Then *you're going to* walk back, sit down, open your tray, and look up at me.") This is a powerful technique that causes students to picture themselves in their mind's eye carrying out your directives. I recommend being as detailed as possible, covering every bit of information or eventuality. Walk them through everything you want them to do, and how you want them to do it, up until the next step.

It's important to note that if your students are doing something for the first time, or if it's early in the school year and they're just getting to know you, then you should model for them after providing your directions. Of course, you can't do this every time you give a direction. There aren't enough hours in the day. Good teaching requires you to be able to give a quick verbal direction and have it followed successfully.

After creating a visualization of what you want accomplished, use the word 'go' to release your students to begin. The 'go' signal is another technique that keeps your students from getting ahead of you mentally or otherwise. It keeps them rooted in the present and actively listening. They can relax in knowing that they don't have to race to get ahead. They can pay attention knowing that you won't allow anyone to start before your signal. Just after your visualization you'll say, "When I say 'go,' you can begin."

This doesn't mean, however, that you're going to release them right away. After another pause to let their mental movie play out, it's a good idea to challenge them by asking, "Is there anyone who doesn't know what to do?" As was mentioned in a previous chapter, what this does is shift responsibility in total from you to them. You've done your job and now it's time for them to do theirs. No one wants to fail after being challenged, and thus you'll find your students straining to do what you ask as best they can.

Occasionally you may have a student ask a clarifying question. This is welcomed and wonderful and you should eagerly answer it. After one more pause and a glance around the room, however, it's now out of your hands. Give your 'go' signal and then watch as your vision plays out before you.

A Chance to Succeed

If in the first moments after giving your 'go' signal your students struggle to follow your directions, that's okay. Resist the urge to jump in and help. Resist the urge to remind and correct and encourage. In the long run they're far better off if you refrain from getting involved. In nearly every circumstance, if you were thorough in your directions, if you used 'you' and 'going to' language, and if you created powerful visualizations, the reason your students are struggling is because in the past they've received too much help.

They have become so accustomed to someone stepping in with reminders that they've lost their ability to do it themselves. They've lost their independence. They've become frozen, unable to transfer the directions you give them into action. This is called learned helplessness, and it's startling how many of today's students suffer from it.

The best way to teach your students that they can indeed do it themselves, that they don't need you or your help, is to fade into the background and let them struggle. That's right.

You're going to step back and observe from a distance as they try to figure out what needs to get done. You're going to let them work their way through the directions you've provided them until they find success on the other side.

If you notice leaders taking over and directing others, this is good. If you see students watching and mimicking others, this is also good. They need to build up their confidence without teacher help first before they can become reliant on themselves. Every time your class successfully works their way through what you've asked them to do without your two cents, they get one step closer to greater independence. They become so used to you giving directions one time and with no reminders that it becomes an expectation. And this makes all the difference. It encourages better listening up front and creates a tenacious mindset that takes pride in a job well done.

When you first use this strategy, your class may very well struggle mightily. They may crash and burn. They may get to the point of failure, to the point where they have no clue how to proceed. It is only at this point that you will step in. But you won't step in by offering reminders. You won't simply call out over the group and tell them where they've gone wrong. You won't lecture, admonish, or criticize. Because remember, it isn't their fault. Somewhere along the line the adults in their life, including their teachers, have done too much for them.

The best way to handle it is to start over from the beginning. Send your students back to their desks, the grandstands, or to wherever they were when you first gave them your directions. Pause again and then give the same directions over again, word for word. This time, they'll get it right and you'll be one step closer to the sharp, independent class you want.

If you can become an expert at giving clear visualizations of your directions, and if you can refrain from stepping in to help, you'll create the kind of go-getter classes that are fun to teach, and that you can do so much with. Once your students become efficient at following simple directions, then make them more complex. Challenge them with more complicated, multi-step directions. Continue pushing them to the limits of their abilities, and you won't believe the transformation from the first day of school to the last.

It's important to note that if your students are struggling to follow directions because one or more of them are goofing around and interfering with the process, then this is a behavior issue and not a listening one. In this case, you would follow the guidelines you'll find in Part Four.

For improving listening, following directions, and independence, however, there isn't a more powerful strategy than presenting spot-on directions and then stepping back and allowing your students to learn how to rely on themselves, to learn how to become competent and trustworthy, and to learn how to approach problems and challenges with determination and confidence.

Observation

B ecause you only see your students once a week, and because they often arrive unprepared to listen intently, it's easy to become a micromanager. It's easy to fall into the trap of guiding and cajoling your students through everything you ask them to do. While the previous chapter focused on becoming too involved in the minutes after giving directions, this chapter will cover the time your students spend working or performing independently.

It's common for specialist teachers to find themselves rushing from one student—or group of students—to the next, reteaching what was taught to the whole class just minutes before. In the same way frequent reminders encourage learned helplessness, reteaching individual students causes them to grow so accustomed to your extra help that they tune you out during your lessons. After all, if they know you'll always be there to reteach them, then what reason do they have to listen the first time? This is often the reason why as soon as you send your students off to practice on their own, hands go up all over the room. Now, this isn't to say that you should refuse to help students who really need it. It's more of an attitude that communicates your belief in them and their abilities.

Part of this attitude comes from you telling them directly that they don't need your help, that they have all the information and know-how they need to practice on their own. Coming from someone they trust and admire, this can have a powerful effect. Ideally, you'll want to stand back and observe, occasionally walking around to look over shoulders, intervening of your own accord when you determine that a word or two could help improve performance. You see, when students work creatively at something on their own, as long as they are headed in the right direction, they become empowered and improvement comes quickly.

When you kneel down to help individuals through something they can readily do themselves, however, when you over-teach and limit their thinking, you communicate to them loud and clear that they indeed *need* your help, that they aren't good enough. You reinforce an untruth that can be detrimental to their development and progress. Furthermore, you become blinded from the needs of the entire group. You're unable to observe the class as a whole, unable to assess where they are and what they need going forward. Helping when they don't need help encourages dependence and helplessness and obscures the feedback you need to adjust your teaching.

The feeling of independence, of working on your craft through your own unique gifts and creativity, is critical for anyone in the arts. Thus, it's important that you provide just enough teaching, just enough scaffolding, for your students to build upon. Present the clear fundamentals and then release them to create.

In an effort to be the kind of teacher who will do anything for their students, too many teachers end up doing too much and stifling creative inspiration, expression, and enjoyment. The very best specialists know when to back off. They know when to slip into the background and let their students explore and progress under their observing eye. As long as your students are working within the spirit by which you instructed them, let them be. They'll not only progress more rapidly, but they'll look forward to coming to your class so much more.

Once your students get used to having ample breathing room, you'll notice fewer hands in the air and fewer students in need of help. This will give you even more freedom to observe and step in when a student strays off course. Behavior, too, will improve as your students get lost in their work, when they know they have a period of independent practice—or partner/group practice—without interference. There is also the benefit that because you're free to observe, you can better manage behavior. You're in better position to witness misbehavior and respond to it before it can disrupt the class. Your watching eyes also make students less inclined to misbehave or stray off topic behind your back. Teachers in the habit of constantly working with individual students have a chaotic room environment for this reason.

Of course, observing more and helping less underscores the importance of having sharp, interesting lessons. It underscores the importance of modeling and checking for understanding before releasing your students to their work. It underscores the importance of setting them up for success.

The combination of vibrant lessons and less individual help can have a transformational effect on your classes and the progress your students make. Bear in mind, however, that knowing when your students really do need your help and knowing when to say merely, "You can do it, I believe in you" is an art that comes from experience.

Part Four:
Rules & Consequences

Classroom Management Plan

The purpose of a classroom management plan is to hold your students accountable for misbehavior. Followed consistently, for every time a student breaks a rule, it also allows you to avoid stressful and potentially hurtful methods of classroom management like yelling, scolding, and lecturing. Instead of taking misbehavior personally or reacting emotionally, instead of creating friction and resentment and fostering dislike, you can lean exclusively on your classroom management plan.

The benefits of handling accountability in this manner are endless and include saving time, safeguarding positive relationships with students, lowering tension and stress, eliminating confusion and misunderstanding, and cutting way down on arguing and confrontation. Combined with your commitment to creating a learning experience your students like and enjoy being part of, it also happens to be the best way to curb misbehavior.

The most effective classroom management plan configuration for specialist teachers is one that is simple—exceedingly so. I recommend just three rules and three consequences.

Rules:
1. Listen and follow directions.
2. Raise your hand.
3. Be nice.

Consequences:
1. Warning
2. Time-out
3. Parents Contacted

These rules and consequences can be interpreted in a number of ways, which is why it's important that you define them for your students. Every student you teach must clearly understand what each of the rules means, what constitutes breaking them, and what exactly happens when they are broken. The meaning and purpose of each of your consequences must also be similarly dissected. I recommend spending 15-20 minutes of the first three or four class periods of the school year thoroughly teaching your plan to your students, including modeling and role-playing the most common scenarios.

You're in effect laying the parameters of a contract between you and your students. In return for following the class rules, you're making a promise to protect their right to learn and enjoy school without interference. You're also promising to handle any and all misbehavior with calm respect and to enforce the consequences to the letter. Otherwise, you risk betraying their trust. You risk creating an atmosphere of resentment and animosity.

Framed in this light, your students will begin to see that your classroom management plan isn't in any way a negative thing. It isn't meant to ruin their fun or rain on their parade. Rather, it's the very thing that ensures their freedom to enjoy your classroom without being bothered, bullied, or interrupted. It matches perfectly your goal of creating a classroom your students look forward to. In fact, it's an important piece of the puzzle, a critical element that allows students to experience the rewards of being in your class.

It is this feeling of enjoying the benefits of being a member of your class that gives your consequences their significance. Consequences matter to students only inasmuch as your class matters to them. For example, time-out only works if participating as a valued member of your class is a more attractive option. If your students dislike being part of your classroom, then your consequences will have little effect.

In the following chapters we'll explain in detail everything you need to know to maximize the power of your classroom management plan. We'll cover what to avoid, what to be wary of, and what to embrace on the road to creating the consistently well-behaved classes you want.

What Not to Do

I t's important at this point to identify two common and
closely linked classroom management approaches you'll
do well to avoid. Both will effectively sabotage your efforts
to create the peaceful teaching and learning experience you
want. The first is any strategy that seeks to *convince* students
to behave. Typically, the way it works is that the teacher will
pull misbehaving students aside to speak to them about their
behavior. They'll counsel and question. They'll cajole and lecture. They'll search for the right words that will somehow per-
suade them to turn from their misbehaving ways.

But the problem with this approach is that it rarely works,
particularly for specialist teachers who may not know their
students very well and thus don't have the rapport to personally influence them. Furthermore, given the popularity of this
approach among teachers, students have learned that if they
can just endure the conference without talking back or being
disrespectful, they can be on their way without a consequence.
You see, for most teachers who use this method, meeting with

the student *is* the consequence. The student tells the teacher what they want to hear and, satisfied, the teacher sends the student along to rejoin the class without any true or meaningful accountability.

The other risk of trying to convince students into improved behavior is that it leads to the second and most detrimental approach you could ever use. It's a strategy of sorts that few teachers feel good about, but of which many use as their primary means of handling misbehavior. It's a strategy most teachers fall into by accident and in response to frustration. Without ever intending to, they find themselves yelling, scolding, berating, using sarcasm, and engaging in other forms of intimidation.

And the thing is, it works. At least initially. Intimidating students can indeed improve behavior in the moment. But it does nothing to actually *change* behavior, and it's remarkably stressful for both you and your students. It creates tension and animosity. It sabotages influential relationships and causes students to dislike being part of your class. And when used in combination with time-out, it causes students to sit and seethe in anger at you instead of reflecting on their mistakes. The other problem is that once you go down this road, it's hard to turn back. It's hard to stop the one thing that works—at least temporarily. For teachers struggling with classroom management, it becomes the lesser of two evils; either they let things go and their room is chaos or they become the mean teacher they never wanted to become and their room is a dark and unhappy place to be.

The solution, as we found in the previous chapter, is to rely exclusively on your classroom management plan. Let it do the heavy lifting for you. Let it remove the emotion, the stress, and the anger that can sprout up when a student blatantly disrupts your class or brazenly disrespects you. Let it take care of holding misbehaving students accountable fairly and effectively while you get on with the business of inspiring your students. Let it do its job, so you can do yours.

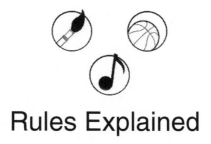

Rules Explained

Your rules should cover every possible misbehavior. In my experience, the three rules I recommend do just that. However, if you feel you need to add a rule—for example, one that addresses taking care of materials and equipment—or change the wording of those recommended, then please do. It shouldn't pose a problem whatsoever. Just remember to keep them simple. You can always define their meaning more specifically for your students.

The first rule I recommend, *Listen and follow directions*, applies only to students who *choose* to break it. In other words, it does not apply to students who either don't hear you or don't understand what you're asking them to do. This is an important distinction. You never want to enforce a consequence unless your students know that their behavior is against the class rules. This underscores the importance of teaching your classroom management plan thoroughly, as well as the importance of utilizing the listening strategies covered in Part Three. There should never be a question as to what constitutes breaking a rule and what doesn't. When they see you approach them to issue a warning or a time-out, they should already know why and what for.

The second rule, *Raise your hand*, is especially important for specialist teachers because we so rarely work with small groups of students. Most of the teaching we do is whole-group instruction, where free participation nearly always leads to chaos. It also shuts out so many students—those who are shy or less assertive—precluding them from participating. Therefore, participation can only be successfully and fairly managed through hand raising. For many of the classes you teach, your students will be used to this approach because so many teachers require it. That doesn't mean, however, that they'll be very good at it. Although it's widely encouraged, it isn't always enforced.

What this means for you is that unless you teach and explain the importance of hand raising, and enforce it consistently, *a lot* of students will call out without raising their hand. They'll interrupt you and each other. They'll compete for airtime and silence those students who need hand raising to gather enough courage to share their thoughts or ask a question. They'll stop the momentum of a lesson like almost nothing else.

Like much of being a specialist teacher, there is some nuance involved in how you decide to enforce this particular rule. In the beginning of the school year, you may want to give two warnings before issuing a time-out, depending on the class you're teaching. Personally, when I'm meeting a class for the first time, particularly if it's kindergarten or first grade, I will allow two warnings for the first three or four weeks.

After that, it's one warning only. You can do this with all of your rules if you like, but for this one in particular it's especially helpful. For some students, calling out is so ingrained that a second chance encourages rather than discourages hand raising.

The final rule, *Be nice*, is admittedly vague. I like it, however, because it covers a great swath of misbehavior. The biggest benefit, though, is that students get it. They understand immediately what it means. Although they may not always be able to articulate it, they all know what being nice looks like. They all know that the rule includes no pushing or hitting or name-calling. They know that it covers yelling at and making fun of others. The rule is so clear that everyone will know when it has been broken, and few students will have the boldness to argue against it. Now, that isn't to say that you don't still need to define it for your students. You do. You still need to model what it looks and sounds like and what is and isn't acceptable. I think you'll find, though, that it is the easiest rule to enforce.

Your rules are designed to cover every misbehavior that could potentially interfere with learning. They form a protective shield that ensures your freedom to teach and your students' freedom to learn. Therefore, they must never be taught as a negative, but rather as something that is good for everyone—something that makes possible the joy of learning a new song, a new art technique, or a new sports game.

Consequences Explained

For classroom teachers, it's best for consequences to be given in straight succession. A warning leads directly to time-out which leads directly to a letter or phone call home to parents. For specialist teachers, however, this isn't the most effective or convenient way to enforce consequences. Doing it this way will likely cause headaches for you, complaints from parents and classroom teachers, and a less effective way to curb misbehavior in your class. The uniqueness of your job calls for a more unique system of giving consequences. The way I recommend is still simple, but allows room for using your best instinct in regard to individual students.

As was mentioned in the previous chapter, in some cases, and with some classes, you may want to afford your students two warnings instead of one depending on age, how well you know the students, and how early it is in the school year. If you have a classroom you're really struggling with and decide to start over from the beginning (more on this in Part Five), you may also want to start out with two warnings. Otherwise, when a student breaks a rule, you'll go directly from the first warning to a time-out—regardless of what rule was broken. In other words, if they receive a warning for not raising their hand and then break a completely different rule several minutes later, they go to time-out. What rule was broken is irrelevant as far as how you enforce your consequences.

When you do send students to time-out, it doesn't matter how far away they are from the rest of the class. So if you don't have a lot of space in your classroom, that's okay. Done right, it shouldn't matter. As long as you have *somewhere* for them to go, it will suffice. A separate desk is optimal, but for music and PE teachers, simply sitting off to the side works as well. An effective time-out consequence is more of a symbolic separation from the class, lesson, or activity they would rather be a part of than it is a physical one. This is where the power of time-out comes from. If the student doesn't feel as if they're missing something, then the time-out will not be effective. It's as simple as that. As covered in Part One, you must have something to offer students that is so compelling that they won't want to miss a minute of class time wasting away in time-out.

While they're sitting in time-out, the expectation is that they sit quietly and watch the lesson. They're required to know what is going on and what their responsibilities are when they return. They may not daydream or play. They must actively listen and be ready to rejoin the class at a moment's notice. With a glance you'll be able to see if this is the case. If it is, you'll invite the student to return to the class in roughly fifteen minutes. If, however, you see the student rolling on the floor or trying to talk to classmates, then you'll leave them where they are. You'll only invite them to return if they can show through their behavior that they want to return. The way you'll do it is to approach and ask, "Would you like to join us?" If they say yes, then wave them in. If not, then turn on your heel and get on with your lesson.

Fifteen minutes may seem like a long time, particularly for primary students, but once again, because you see your students only once per week you don't have the luxury to send anything but a strong message. It's the perfect amount of time for them to reflect on their misbehavior and fully comprehend what they're missing. It also frames any interruption to learning and enjoying school in a serious light. Too many teachers fail to communicate how detrimental misbehavior is and how profoundly it affects not only the student in question, but every other member of the community.

Given the detail and the specific expectations of students, this process of giving and receiving consequences must be thoroughly explained and modeled for your students as part of the series of classroom management lessons you'll provide during the first few weeks of school. It isn't fair to them, nor will it be very effective, if they don't fully understand the process.

If you've invited a student to rejoin the class, they're working with two strikes against them. However, if they break a rule for a third time, you won't automatically proceed to the third consequence. Instead, you will send them back to time-out for the rest of the period. There are a couple of reasons for this. For a specialist teacher, trying to get ahold of several parents or more per week is a logistical nightmare. The other problem is that often there is little if any history between you and the parent. You'll want to know in the very least how successful previous contact home has been and if there are any issues you need to be aware of before calling or sending a behavior letter.

Another reason for not contacting parents immediately is because I've found that some students need a second time-out to receive your strong message. Remember, you won't always know your students very well or whether or not—or how well—they're being held accountable at home or in their regular classroom. Being asked to prove themselves, to show that they're truly taking responsibility for their poor behavior, might be an entirely new experience for them.

When the class period ends, don't release the student from time-out just yet. Wait until every student is lined up and ready to go, then ask them to join the group. This way you avoid the possibility for misbehavior in the final minute of your class, leaving no time for accountability.

So when should you implement the third consequence? I recommend using it when misbehavior becomes a pattern. When you notice that the same student is spending parts of each week in time-out, you have an obligation to contact parents. They have a right to know when their child is misbehaving to a degree that they're unable to right the ship on their own.

There are two possibilities when contacting parents: a phone call, or a letter given to the student to take home. A letter is more effective and more powerful because it adds another layer of accountability. The student has to *do* something to account for their misbehavior. They have to be responsible for keeping track of the letter, delivering it to their parents, explaining their behavior, asking for it to be signed, and then returning it to you the next day. You'll find that when students are able to do this, they'll rarely cause trouble in your classroom again.

I only recommend this method, however, if you've been at the same school for a number of years and are willing to follow through and see it to the end. Sometimes it takes a lot of extra work. You may have to call parents to give them a heads up that the letter is coming home. You may have to give the student multiple copies, check to make sure it's in their backpack, show up at their classroom door every morning, etc. It can be an involved process, but it can also be remarkably effective.

The best kind of letter to send home is a form letter briefly explaining the importance of following rules in your classroom followed by a check off list of rules that were broken. You want the letter to prompt questions from the parent that only the student can answer. Again, though, you want to know information about the parent(s) and how supportive they are before trying this strategy. Admittedly, it isn't for everyone. But if you're an experienced teacher and have a good reputation among the parents in the community, it can be especially powerful.

The other option is a simple phone call home. If you choose this method, it's best to stick to the facts. Just tell the parent what behaviors you've been seeing and what you've done to hold their child accountable. It's an informational conversation. What they do with the information is up to them. I've found this method to be most helpful to parents, who will appreciate your non-judgmental attitude and will be more than willing to do what they can at home to help. Furthermore, because you've stuck to your classroom management plan and haven't engaged in yelling, chewing out, and the like, you're able to contact parents with confidence knowing that you've treated their child with the utmost respect.

However behavior plays out in your classroom in any given week or class, all is forgotten by the next week. Every new class period is a chance to get it right. All consequences are wiped clean and every student gets the opportunity to get it right, to start fresh, as if it's the first day of school.

Giving Consequences

How you give a consequence in response to rule-breaking makes a big difference in how well it eliminates future misbehavior. There is much misunderstanding on this topic, with most teachers enforcing consequences without giving any thought as to how it should be done. Typically, consequences are meted out with an air of intimidation. They're delivered with a glare, a lecture, or a stern rebuke. There is an element of fear involved, a feeling of "how dare you interrupt my classroom."

But the problem with this approach is that it interferes with the accountability process and misrepresents the true purpose of your classroom management plan. It sends the message that you're angry with them instead of sending the message that results in improved behavior. You see, if the way you give a consequence creates friction, animosity, or resentment, then instead of reflecting on their misbehavior and taking responsibility for it, they'll stew in anger at you.

The whole reason they received a warning or had to go to time-out in the first place is lost in the bad blood and distrust between you.

The purpose of your classroom management plan is to protect each student's right to learn and enjoy being part of your class. It's a positive, not a negative. It's meant to free them to enjoy the wonderful benefits of being a valued member of your class. Therefore, it's *never* personal. To be effective, you must be able to separate the misbehavior from the student. You must never let their misbehavior, no matter how egregious, taint your relationship with them.

I realize that this can be easier said than done. It's easy to lose your cool and at times there is no small amount of satisfaction in castigating a student up one wall and down the other. And maybe they even deserve it. But managing your classroom based on fear and coercion is exhausting, terribly stressful, and hurtful to students. It will pull you ever closer to burnout every day. To top it off, it isn't very effective.

Simply knowing that you can rely exclusively on your classroom management plan, however, and that you don't have to try and convince or intimidate your students into behaving, will give you more than enough confidence not to react emotionally to misbehavior. You can relax in knowing that a calm, even clinical, approach will *always* work better in the long run. For many teachers, this revelation can be life-changing. From one day to the next, they go from stressed and ready to pull their hair out to calm and excited to teach.

The most effective way to give a consequence is just about as simple as you can imagine. It's also fast, taking up very little class time. As we've learned in previous chapters, the first consequence is a warning. A warning is a consequence in name only. In reality, it's a courtesy you provide your students. It's a declaration of free grace you offer by letting them know that you're aware a rule has been broken, but that no real consequence is forthcoming. Therefore, when a student breaks a rule for the first time in a given class period, you approach calmly and say, "You have a warning because . . ." and then briefly state the infraction and what rule was broken. Now, if the transgression is obvious, like calling out without raising their hand, then you can skip this part. In this case, a simple "You have a warning" will suffice. Then turn and walk away. Don't wait for a response or an explanation. Nothing else needs to be said.

Now it's important that when you first teach your classroom management plan that you explain to your students that a warning doesn't mean they're in trouble. It just means that they're one step (or two steps) away from time-out. This understanding makes a difference in how effective your warnings will be. Viewed in this light, your students will see a warning as an opportunity to take responsibility, to learn from their mistakes, and to resolve not to trigger the next consequence. They'll only make these connections, however, if you refrain from lecturing, scolding, or creating friction. Just deliver your warning calmly and matter-of-factly and be on your way. It bears mentioning that you should also avoid trying to describe to students how they should feel and what they should think about their misbehavior. This is another common error that undermines the power of self-reflection and responsibility.

If the same student breaks another rule within the same class period, you'll approach and speak to the student in the same calm manner you did when giving the warning. "Please walk to the time-out area because you broke rule number three and didn't keep your hands to yourself." Again, you'll turn and walk away. You will, of course, glance over to make sure the student is heading to time-out, but you won't escort them there. Leading a student to time-out increases the chance that they'll argue with you or refuse to go. If the student remains quiet and attentive in time-out, after fifteen minutes walk over with a smile and say, "Would you like to join us?" If the student responds affirmatively, then welcome them back with open arms. Once the student fulfills their responsibility, the consequence is over and the student can rejoin the class and its good graces, with no strings attached.

Sending a letter home is also a quick and painless process. If one particular student has been a problem for three or four weeks running and you've determined that a note home would be better than a phone call, then at the end of the class period, when your class is lined up and waiting for their classroom teacher, you'll simply hand the student the letter and say, "Please have this signed and returned to me tomorrow." Again, don't wait for a response or an argument. If, however, you don't know anything about the child's parents and want to call home instead, then be sure and tell the student ahead of time.

Handling consequences in this low stress, hands-off manner has the powerful effect of heaping 100% of the responsibility on the misbehaving student's shoulders. They are left with no one to blame, no one to get angry at, and nowhere else to point the finger but at themselves. They may not be happy about going to time-out or getting a letter to take home, but in their heart they'll know it's because of what they did, not what you did. And this makes all the difference.

Being Consistent

A sk one hundred teachers and ninety-nine of them will tell you that being consistent with your classroom management plan is important. Few, however, actually are consistent. The truth is, it's an area most teachers struggle with. They know they need to follow through every time a rule is broken, but doing so can be a challenge.

Sometimes it just seems easier to let things go—if the misbehavior isn't serious, for example, or if the offending student rarely misbehaves, or if you're right in the middle of something important. Other times you may not be in the mood to confront a difficult student or sift through an incident involving multiple students. These are all valid reasons, to be sure, but they don't change the fact that inconsistency makes managing your class more difficult. Being wishy-washy or picking and choosing when to enforce a consequence will lead to more frequent and more severe misbehavior.

Inconsistency is unfair, and students are quick to pick up on it. *Why does she get away with calling out and I don't? Why is he allowed to push in line and I get a warning for it?* Why indeed? It also communicates to students that you don't really mean what you say and therefore can't be trusted. It causes them to look at you with skepticism, confusion, and frustration. It shouts from the rooftops that you're not a leader they can believe in.

Typically, a new school year starts out with so much hope. But as soon as you begin looking the other way in the face of misbehavior, things will deteriorate quickly. Your classes will test you and push your buttons. They'll become emboldened with disrespect. Your voice and presence will carry less weight and relevance. And when you *do* try to enforce a consequence, your students will react with aggressive pushback. They'll complain and carry on because you've shown a propensity to give in and not be a person of your word. Any effort, then, to rein them in, to get tough in response, will be met with rebellion.

The many messages you send to your students when you say you have a classroom management plan, when you say you have high expectations, and when you say you'll protect their right to learn, but don't follow through, can be disastrous. The sad result is that because you're left with no other recourse, it's difficult, if not impossible, to avoid falling into hurtful habits like berating, scolding, and harshly criticizing your students. You'll see them as an adversary rather than an eager ally looking for leadership.

If there is a secret to being consistent, it's the understanding of just how important it is. It's knowing that when you follow through on your promises, good things happen. Your students will respect you, trust you, listen to you, and look up to you. Your classroom management plan will work as it should. Your words will line up with your actions and you'll be a teacher of integrity. A semi-adherence to your rules and consequences, on the other hand, will never work. You have to be all in, no matter the misbehavior, the identity of the offending student, or how difficult it seems in the moment.

The good news is that it's easier to be consistent as a specialist teacher. Because every class period is a new beginning, and because you may not know all of your students so well, there are fewer obstacles and fewer variables to be concerned with. You can focus your energy on delivering first-class lessons and creating a class your students look forward to. You can relax in the certainty that your classroom management plan will safeguard their right to learn and enjoy a subject you're passionate about. You can teach with freedom knowing that you don't have to yell or rant or convince your students to behave, but that you and your students have the protection of a fair and faithfully followed classroom management plan.

Every Day is a New Day

An essential characteristic of effective classroom management is that all misbehavior and subsequent consequences are wiped clean at the end of every class period— meaning that the next time you see your students, they have the benefit of a fresh start. They have another chance to get it right, another chance to listen, learn, behave, and be successful. Now, this isn't just another strategy. It must be your abiding philosophy. It must be your mantra not only when it comes to your classroom management plan, but also in regard to your relationship with students.

As mentioned in previous chapters, it's important to avoid causing friction with your students. It's important they like you and trust you. To that end, you can never let any one student or classroom so get under your skin that you begin to hold a grudge. You must ignore any and all past transgressions and *choose* to enjoy teaching them and getting to know them better. You see, if you let animosity take hold, it will bubble to the surface in one form or another. Despite your best efforts to conceal these feelings, your students will find you out. They'll know if you dislike them or are annoyed by them and will respond in kind. By the same token, allowing your consequences to do their job safeguards positive and influential relationships with your students.

This is especially true for your most difficult students, who are used to being disliked by teachers—which is why it can be so difficult to win them over and to earn their trust. They assume you'll be like all the rest. They assume that you'll grow so tired of them that you couldn't possibly see the good in them. What this does is further label them a "problem" and makes it all the more difficult to build the rapport you need to help them veer off the path they're on and choose behavior that is needed for success in school.

When you invite a student to rejoin your class after being in time-out, you must do so with no strings attached. You must do so with no reminders, threats, or glares. It's a free pass. They're welcomed back in good standing with the same benefits afforded any other member of your class. That includes your smiles, your jokes, and your friendly banter. It includes total absolution, complete grace, and nothing owed. If your students fulfill their responsibilities while in time-out, if they sit quietly and attentively, then they're truly free.

This knowledge alone can be a game-changer for your most difficult students. For it has the power to soothe bitter, vengeful hearts, melt away heavily fortified walls of distrust, and transform them into everyday members of your class. They'll so appreciate you and want to please you that even if they're still a terror in their own classroom, they'll behave for you. It's in your positive relationships that the secrets of managing difficult students reside. It's in your forgiveness, your refusal to hold a grudge, and your steadfast belief in the power of an individual to change, to grow, and to turn from their misbehaving ways that makes the difference.

Possessing the core conviction that every day is a new day for your students is also a remarkable de-stressor and a much more pleasant way to run your classroom. Although it's meant to be used with every student and throughout all of your classes, through its transformational power you'll find your most challenging students to be the greatest beneficiary, as well as the source of your deepest fulfillment and satisfaction.

Referring Students

Only dangerous behavior like bullying, threatening, or fighting warrants referring a student to your principal. Otherwise, you should handle the problem yourself. The main reason for this is that allowing someone else to take care of misbehavior for you weakens your ability to manage your class. It communicates to students that you're not the ultimate authority, which emboldens them to misbehave all the more. It encourages them to push your buttons and probe the boundaries of your patience. It causes them to have less respect for you and fewer reasons to listen to what you say.

Passing a student off to someone else will also affect your confidence. It will make you question your ability to handle difficult students and classrooms and highly disruptive situations. It will cause you to be shaky and tentative and your classroom management plan to be muddled and unclear. Your students need to know that you're in control. They need to see you efficiently handling misbehavior and holding those responsible for disruptions to your high standards. If you show you're unsure of yourself, your students will nonchalantly ignore you and your instruction. They'll turn and talk to a neighbor in the middle of your lessons. They'll flaunt misbehavior right in front of you, just daring you to do something about it.

The same is true if you fail again and again to follow your classroom management plan or if you send a student back to their classroom teacher or down to the office. Any action that exposes you as indecisive, uncertain, or lacking in confidence will result in a weakening ability to manage your class. Strong leadership presence is especially important for art, music, and PE teachers who often have to prove that they're a real teacher who teaches a real class.

Taking care of your own misbehavior is a statement to your students. It engenders trust and confidence in you and proves to them that you're a leader worth following. It gives you and the words you use more weight and relevance. By the same token, it's also a statement to your administrator that you're competent and that you've got it covered. Specialist teachers have a reputation for struggling with classroom management. The reason, though, isn't because there is some missing quality inherent in those who pursue art, music, and PE teaching. Rather, it's because managing behavior as a specialist is more difficult. It's a great challenge to see 20 or more classes per week. But not everyone will understand this or know any better.

This highlights the importance of being an expert in classroom management and taking care of misbehavior on your own. The good news is that now you know how. Now you know exactly what to do in response to every act of misbehavior. As soon as it pops up on your radar, you calmly and clearly enforce a consequence. Then you continue on with your lesson as if nothing happened.

Part Five:
Bad Days & Tough Classes

Slow Down

O ne of the best things you can do to avoid a bad day is to simply slow down. As covered in a previous chapter, it's a good idea to meet your students outside of your classroom, music room, or gymnasium and assess how prepared they are to learn. For your most challenging classes this strategy is especially important. If they're antsy and restless or loud and squirrelly in line, calmly ask for their attention and then stand and wait. Allow them a moment to settle down and shake the excitability from their limbs. Breathe deeply and let your calm presence fill the air around them.

Once they're calm and quiet, review your expectations for the first routine. Remind them that there is a point riding on how well they enter the room. You'll also want to preview your lesson, explaining how fun or interesting or otherwise compelling it is. Pause again and wait until they're settled and quiet before giving the signal to enter the room. If one or two students break a rule as they're walking in, then enforce a consequence on the spot. If most of the group enters in any way unlike how you first modeled the routine, then wait until they sit down and are quiet before sending them back outside to try again.

The idea is to gain control immediately—before it gets out of hand. Only proceed when your class is giving you what you want. You don't have to get upset and lecture, and you don't have to repeat your expectations. Simply stay calm and move forward with your instruction only when they're ready. If they're not, just wait. You have to be willing to wait out the entire period if you have to. In all likelihood this is never going to happen. It's your willingness to do so, however, that makes the strategy work. Having this as a possibility in the back of your mind will show outwardly in the way you speak and move and carry yourself, which in turn makes a difference in how your students respond.

If you start slow every week with all of your classes, and proceed only to the degree that they're ready, they'll grow accustomed to it—in a good way. They'll calm down quicker and be more prepared from week to week. They'll flip the switch from excitability to peaceful focus. They'll know that when they're with you, the lessons and activities are cool and the learning is fun, but that they too have a part to play. Your class is a two-way street. You give your best for them. You create great lessons and give them the freedom they crave to learn and explore. But they have to give their best for you also. They have to be prepared to behave. They have to be respectful and pleasant and eager to listen. They have to prove themselves ready to move on from one moment, one activity, and one transition to the next.

By taking it slow and assessing your students from the beginning, you avoid losing control. You avoid blowups, severe misbehavior, and stressful class periods. You're able to take the most difficult class in the school, dropped off at your door wild, restless, and out of control, and return them happy and calm and looking forward to next week.

Do it Again

The do-it-again strategy bridges the gap between the previous chapter and the one to follow. In this scenario, you give a direction or commence with a routine and your previously well-behaved students completely blow it. In other words, despite being calm and attentive just seconds before, they fight over their paintbrushes, play with the PE equipment instead of cleaning up, or enter the music room like a troop of Howler monkeys. It's an isolated incident, one that if you let pass without a response this one time wouldn't be such a big deal. In all likelihood you would be able to get them back on track without too much trouble.

Most teachers, though, would call them on it. They would remind them of how they should have followed directions and why such behavior was unacceptable. They may even give a loud and angry lecture. But effective classroom management is about action. It's less about what you say and more about what you do. The truth is, the long-term difference in effectiveness between letting such an incident go without a response and berating students with a red-faced lecture wouldn't be much.

To send a message that will have an impact beyond the rest of the class period, you would allow your students to finish the routine or direction, and then send them right back to do it over again. You wouldn't continue on with your day, even if you're pressed for time. The only exception would be the last minute of the period, in which case you would start their class the following week by revisiting the incident and repeating it then.

Requiring students to repeat poorly followed directions correctly is one of your most powerful and reliable tools, helping you avoid so many problems and misbehaviors in the future. It keeps your students sharp and acts as a constant reminder that all routines and directions must be followed as taught. It can certainly be a nuisance to ask your students to line up again, for example. But the ability to give a direction and have it followed without drama and misbehavior is *everything* to a specialist teacher. It keeps your class running smoothly and allows both you and your students to focus on what matters.

Now, when you decide that a direction or routine should be repeated, wait until your students are quiet and attentive before sending them back. A common mistake is to try to stop students mid-routine. *"No, no, no! You know that's not how you do it. Now go back and try it again. And this time, walk!"* What this does is make you look like a grouchy and unlikeable complainer. Your students will then grudgingly repeat the process, grumbling under their breath at how unfair you are. For the strategy to be effective your students must see that the responsibility lies with them. If they're angry with you, then it becomes less impactful.

It's important to note that if only a small number of students stray from your directions, you would enforce a consequence rather than having everyone do it again, which in most circumstances is how it will go. Rarely will you have half the class do it perfectly and the other half poorly. It's usually either just a few students or nearly the whole class, which makes your decision to enforce or redo an easy one. If it does happen, however, if you do have half or a third of your class perform a routine poorly, it's okay to have just those students do it again.

If you employ this strategy for every time your students fail to follow your directions or a routine as taught, then it will stop happening. They'll stop wasting time and goofing around. They'll stop the behaviors that drive you crazy. When they know that you'll back up your words with action, they'll follow your directives out of habit. It's not so much a threat hanging over their heads, but rather a voice in the back of their minds reminding them of your expectations.

Your students have to recall from week to week what you expect, which isn't easy given that they may have a different set of expectations in their home classroom. The moment they see you they have to immediately adjust to how you do things. And the only way that can happen is through your consistent actions.

Restart

A common problem for many specialist teachers is that they don't recognize when they've lost control of their class. They raise their voice and talk over students. They repeat themselves over and over again. They perpetually remind, warn, and threaten. Yet they keep at it day after day, assuming that it's just the way things are, that it's just how students behave in that particular school or neighborhood. It's an approach to classroom management based on hope, on the false belief that the students, and the make up of each class, determine whether they have a good teaching experience or not. But the truth is, as teachers, we decide. We control how well behaved our classes are.

The first step is to realize when the train has jumped the tracks. If you find yourself frustrated and stressed out and calling out over the din of your classroom, then you've lost control. And you need to do something about it right away. The longer you wait, the more difficult it will be to get the train back on track. You have to be willing, however, to make a wholesale change in the way you're doing things now and start anew. The good news is that you can push the restart button on classroom management anytime you like, even while in the middle of a lesson.

You first need to acquire your students' quiet attention, which for some teachers may be no easy task. It may mean that you have to shoo your students one at a time to their seats. You may have to repeat yourself a dozen times. You may have to wait five, ten, or even fifteen minutes until they're quiet and looking at you. Whatever it is, you must be willing to do it. You can't start over until you gain a base level control.

Once your students are quiet and looking at you, you can begin the work of transforming your class from unruly and disrespectful to attentive and eager to learn. The key is to practice doing one thing well. I recommend a simple routine like lining up and leaving the room. The teamwork, behavior, and discipline required to line up is the same needed to successfully perform virtually every other routine, procedure, or direction you give.

Referring back to the chapter on teaching routines in Part Two, you're going to thoroughly teach, model, and then practice how to line up and exit the room as if it were the first day of school. Calmly and patiently show your students in a highly detailed way precisely what you expect them to do. Take your time and don't hold back or settle for anything less than what you want. Have several individual students practice first before allowing the whole group to practice. Observe closely, and if they mess up or make a mistake, stop them immediately and have them do it again. Unlike an earlier chapter in Part Five, you mustn't allow them to finish the routine unless it's perfect. With a class that is out of control, you want to stop them *before* they have a chance to become unruly and chaotic.

When you're happy and satisfied with how your students are lining up and exiting the room, then review your classroom management plan in a similarly detailed manner. In a sense, you're starting over from scratch, reteaching the basic behavior skills needed for your students to succeed and enjoy your class. It's an intervention of sorts. It only works, however, if you're willing to see it through. It only works if the next time you have the same class (or classes), you hold them accountable, both with your classroom management plan for individual students and the do-it-again strategy for the entire class.

Because you often don't know what habits your students are learning in their home classroom, classroom management for specialist teachers is a week after week, period after period commitment to your word. It entails showing your students what you expect and then holding them to it. This is the key to never losing control in the first place and always leaving for the day content, relaxed, and knowing that you provided the best learning environment for your students.

The Catalysts

Although your students are solely responsible for their behavior, most bad days are unwittingly caused by the teacher. Tension, unpreparedness, and inconsistency are catalysts for unruliness, disrespect, and misbehavior. They create resentment and excitability. They bring about a dislike of you and being a member of your classroom. They weaken your influence and cause you to fall into bad habits like yelling, complaining, and taking misbehavior personally.

Before greeting your students, no matter how frazzled or frustrated you're feeling, you must never let it show. Even if you have only 30 seconds between classes, use the time to take a few deep breaths and shake the tension from your body. Remind yourself that how you present yourself to your students makes a monumental difference in how they behave. Decide that for the entire period, no matter what happens, you will maintain a calm, even composure.

Speak in a soft, soothing voice. Move gracefully. Smile and tell your students how glad you are to see them. Set the tone for the day by modeling the calm but focused behavior you want from them. They'll pick up on your vibe and follow your cue if only you give them the chance. Remember, it pays to stop your class before they enter your room in order to help eliminate excitability and offer a preview of the lesson. This is the moment that so often determines how well your students will do that day. You never want to rush it.

It can be a challenge, however, to act so easygoing when you're feeling unprepared. The short window of time between classes makes it rare for specialist teachers to ever feel completely ready. Certainly you want to be as prepared as you can, but you have to be realistic. It doesn't matter how long you've been teaching, you'll always feel not-quite prepared for your students. It's normal and something you can't let bother you. You can't let it fluster you in front of your students or cause you to lose focus.

The best specialist teachers are able to fake it. They're able to present a great lesson while being calm and funny and seemingly totally prepared. Relying on your students and the routines you've thoroughly taught them will help you take care of setting up equipment and materials and cleaning up at the end of the period. A hyper-focus on your objectives and what you want your students to be able to do at the end of your lesson also helps to keep you on track.

Finally, it's your consistency in responding to misbehavior that helps you avoid bad days. That first warning you give each period sends a message to the rest of the class that it's business as usual, that no matter what is going on at school or in the world, whether it be record snowfall or Halloween or a total Lunar eclipse, nothing has changed. You're the same teacher this week as you were the week before. Your consistency in manner, voice, and personality, particularly in the opening minutes of the period, will put your students at ease, settle them down, and allow them to relax and focus on learning.

Part Six:
Final Words

Presence

There exists a cadre of specialist teachers who are able to command effortless respect and polite behavior from their students. There is something about them, something unique in the way they carry themselves that causes students to behave differently around them. It's as if they possess an innate energy or vibe that calms, matures, and sweeps unruliness from the classroom. Both they and their students can feel this vibe palpably. And both know the other feels it too. It's an unspoken reality—accepted and readily acknowledged. *"Mrs. Decker? Oh, yes, we behave in her classroom."*

Notice that it isn't *"we **have** to behave in her classroom."* It is simply that they do, matter-of-factly. Just the way it is. Now this vibe, which is more tangibly described as a presence, doesn't come from anything these teachers do on the outside. It's not in the way they dress, the way they look, or the way they move in particular that gives them their superior influence. Rather, it comes from a deep-seated belief they carry with them on the inside, which gives them a level of confidence, calmness, and freedom that eludes most of their colleagues. It's a secret of sorts that has an almost supernatural effect on students. But it is very real. So real, in fact, that you'll know right away when you have it. It's a feeling of empowerment, a *knowing* that you hold the upper hand in the relationship.

That isn't to say that the teacher-student relationship is a battle for control. It's not—or shouldn't be. It's just that in classrooms, music rooms, and gymnasiums where the teacher struggles with classroom management, the students carry the balance of power in the relationship. Having presence, however, shifts this power—and the leverage to effectively manage your classroom—to you, automatically and without effort. So how do you acquire this presence?

The answer is simple and can be broken down into two distinct but seemingly opposite attitudes. The first is that you have to care deeply about your students. So deeply, in fact, that you're willing to forego all short-term strategies—those that so many teachers rely on daily, even hourly—in favor of classroom management principles that are best for students and proven to work for the long haul. Most teachers can readily grasp this first attitude. Caring deeply about students comes naturally to those who have dedicated their careers to helping children. It's the second attitude that gives them pause.

The second attitude can be harder at first to wrap your head around, but once it becomes part of who you are, it will change *everything*. It is this: From the moment your students arrive at your classroom door, until they leave, you mustn't care if they misbehave. To put another way, when your students misbehave, you can't let it affect you emotionally. You can't let it bother you, get under your skin, or disrupt your enjoyment of the day. Not one iota.

Now the only way to get to this point is to recall the first attitude—caring enough for your students long-term success and well being that you only rely on principles, strategies, and solutions that are best for them.

Thus, you must no longer rely on false praise, yelling, scolding, lecturing, questioning, glaring, pleading, eye-rolling, bribery, intimidation, or any other temporary or reactionary method that harms, manipulates, or creates friction with students. Instead, you must consistently follow your classroom management plan—which allows you to hold students accountable for misbehavior while keeping your ever-growing influential and trusting relationship with them intact.

To care without caring will fill you with a gentle but strong leadership presence your students will respect and love you for. They'll appreciate that your promise to protect their right to learn and enjoy school (by following your classroom management plan) isn't personal. But rather, it's an act of compassion and responsibility, of growth and reflection, and of imparting life lessons. This rare combination of deep care with seemingly no care at all will transform your class from one that is extrinsically motivated to behave—which is weak and temporary—to one that is intrinsically motivated, which is real and lasting and unstoppable.

A Love for Your Class

I f you were to have only one goal this coming school year, make it that your students enjoy being in your class. Because no strategy, technique, or method in the world works as well to motivate students to behave, attend during lessons, and focus on their creative work. Instilling a love for school affects and changes students like nothing else can or ever will, improving the effectiveness of virtually everything you do. It can turn around the most difficult student, set fire under the most uninspired, and change a negative outlook from drab and demoralized to bright and expectant.

For many specialist teachers, *this* is the missing ingredient. Your curriculum is important, to be sure, but it belongs in the second fiddle section of your orchestra, while cultivating a love and appreciation of school and being part of your classroom takes spotlight on center stage. It's the attitude and enthusiasm and want-to in your students, after all, that opens them to learning and makes your curriculum go. It's the heady joy of being in a class they can't wait to get to that leads to inspiration, exploration, and curiosity.

If your students aren't happy coming to your class, if they don't look forward to seeing you and engaging with their classmates, if your lessons are yawn-inducing and your personality is flat, then *everything* bogs down. Everything stumbles and grinds and grows increasingly more difficult as the school year wears on. The unavoidable truth is that when boredom and dissatisfaction take root, your students will create their own enjoyment. They'll look for their own stimulation outside of the parameters of your class. They'll choose to make their own fun instead of listening and embracing your instruction. Like poison ivy amid the world's changing climates, disrespect and misbehavior thrive in such an environment.

The good news is that creating a classroom your students look forward to isn't difficult, nor does it need to be a great sacrifice. It doesn't take extra planning. You don't have to wow them with your acting and oratory skills. And every lesson doesn't have to be an exhilarating roller coaster ride. It is simply an attitude, a spirit, and a cultivation of enjoyment. It's finding humor in the everyday and laughter for laughter's sake. It's the relationships, the shared moments of discovery, and the sheer pleasure of teaching and learning something interesting. It's in your smile. It's in your tone of voice. It's in your actions and movements, your body language, and your commitment to creating a culture of appreciation—starting with you and playing forward around the room and back again, to and from every student. It is your enthusiasm for *teaching*. Not the job of teaching, mind you, and not the idea of teaching, but the real heart of the matter, the imparting of knowledge, the simple rewards of showing your students something they haven't experienced before.

So many teachers lose track of this. They lose track of where the true joy of teaching resides and of why they became a teacher in the first place. They lose track of themselves in the acres of *stuff* that conspire to sap the pure satisfaction of inspiring young minds. The sad result is that the life and vitality of the classroom, music room, or gymnasium becomes lost in a forest of peripherals. It becomes lost in all the schedules and meetings and materials and trainings and the other less importants.

But only if you let it. Be well prepared before beginning each day of school, absolutely. But keep your focus on your students. Keep your focus on the **act of teaching**, on the celebration of teaching, on creating a learning experience your students love being part of. Because when you cultivate a love of school first, everything else—from classroom management to motivation to inspired, unforgettable learning . . . clicks into place.

The Freedom to Teach

When I became a PE teacher after so many years in the classroom, I had no idea what I was getting myself into. I can remember being taken aback by the behaviors I witnessed during that first week on the job. It seemed I could hardly finish a sentence without being interrupted, and the students were more interested in the occasional bee buzzing by than anything I had to say.

Little did I know that it was the beginning of a journey I wouldn't trade for anything in the world. The joy of teaching a subject I'm passionate about has been a great blessing. I know, however, that I must always be on top of my game. Although there is great freedom to teach from your heart and to let your creativity sing, being a specialist teacher doesn't allow for a seat-of-your-pants approach to classroom management. Not even for a single day.

It takes a minute-by-minute commitment to the principles, strategies, and solutions that are proven to work regardless of where you teach or how many students you see every week. It takes the same steady drip, drip, drip accountability of a well-taught classroom management plan, an adherence to routines and procedures that save time and keep students focused, and the creation of a learning environment your students can't wait to get to every day.

Despite class after class showing up at your door unprepared to listen and learn, despite teaching multiple grade levels per day, despite at times having little or no transition time between periods and trying to learn the names of 400-600 students, managing behavior as a specialist teacher doesn't have to be a burden. It doesn't have to be stressful or time-consuming. It doesn't have to be difficult, confrontational, or filled with dread.

The approach to classroom management described on these pages was designed specifically for specialist teachers like you to set you free of the many frustrations of day-in and day-out poor behavior, inattentiveness, and disrespect. It was honed and tested over many years in some of the most difficult teaching situations imaginable. Although you'll still have challenging moments, and classes you'll have to take your time with, I'm convinced that if you put what you learn into practice, you can have the teaching experience you desire.

You can turn your focus away from the negativity, the confrontations, and the battles, and toward the wonderful rewards of being a specialist teacher. You're free, after all. You're free to teach, to inspire, to let loose your unique talents and gifts upon the next generation.

You're free to laugh and to love and to impact your students for a lifetime.

For more tips, strategies, and solutions,
visit smartclassroommanagement.com

Made in the USA
Middletown, DE
14 August 2015